THE POWER OF THE PROVISIONAL

THE POWER OF THE PROVISIONAL

by

ROGER SCHUTZ
Prior of Taizé

Translated by
PHILIP PARSONS AND TIMOTHY WILSON

HODDER AND STOUGHTON

English translation copyright © 1969 by Hodder
and Stoughton

First printed 1969

SBN 340 02544 1

Originally published in France by Les Presses de
Taizé, under the title *Dynamique du Provisoire*, ©
1965 by Les Presses de Taize (S.-et-L.) France.

Printed in Great Britain for Hodder and Stoughton
Limited, St. Paul's House, Warwick Lane, London,
E.C.4 by Cox & Wyman Limited, London, Reading
and Fakenham.

CONTENTS

	page
TOWARDS A NEW DIMENSION OF ECUMENISM	8
Ecumenism has remained confined	8
Ways open to us	10
Back to the sources of the contemplative life	12
AVOIDING THE SPLIT BETWEEN GENERATIONS	15
Coming to terms with today	15
The thirst for fulfilment	17
Rediscovering the Gospel	19
Common creation	21
MEETING THOSE WHO CANNOT BELIEVE	24
Ecumenism a prerequisite	24
Dialogue with all men	26
IDENTIFYING OURSELVES WITH THE POOR OF THE WORLD	30
Poverty without charity, shadow without light	30
The first Beatitude in action	33
Living the spirit of poverty	35
Towards a social doctrine of ecumenism	37

LIVING THE MYSTERY OF THE CHURCH   41
Accepting the institutions of the Church   41
Authority, an element of unity   45
Solidarity with all who are baptised   47
Advance, not flight   51
Putting an end to the schism   57
Woven into history   60

LIVING IN CONTEMPLATIVE EXPECTATION
OF GOD   66
Awaiting and provisional   66
Hold on in serenity   69
Bearers of ecumenicity   72
Intimacy and solitude   74
Contemplative expectation   75

NOTES   80

The vocation of the Reformation, when it began, lay in dependence on the provisional in face of what it wanted to reform; an event which burst forth from the heart of the old institutions.

Ecumenism can only survive today if there is a dynamism which drives it to explore ever new dimensions. Otherwise the ecumenical movement will collapse instead of winning more and more Christians, and through them, all men.

Faced as we are with the rapid pace of development, the power which comes from accepting the provisional allows us greater freedom the more we are faithful to the essentials; and this always offers us a chance to take breath.

TOWARDS A NEW DIMENSION
OF ECUMENISM

Ecumenism has remained confined

TODAY the rising tide of the ecumenical movement is raising immense hopes. What is to be done so that the flood, far from subsiding, gradually gains momentum? It is more urgent than ever that we use every possible means to give ecumenism a new dimension.

Ecumenism is the attempt to make visible the unity in brotherhood of the baptised, without humiliating anyone, though in a spirit of humility. This is a particularly delicate mission, which requires the resources of the whole person. A partial commitment is not enough.

Ecumenism was born in the West in very restricted groups, which tried to awaken the Christian conscience to a situation which is intolerable for anyone who professes to love his brother. Branded by its Western origins, instead of attaining that universality which rightly belongs to it, it has remained limited in dimension. In particular, it has done little to link us with

Christians of the southern hemisphere. Moreover it came into being in a pluralistic society where the witness of Christians, already limited, is still further diminished because of their disunity.

If the flood of ecumenism, now at its height, is directed only into channels set by certain Churchmen in positions of responsibility, it will no longer have the force to catch up the younger generations who are coming more and more to dread anything which bears the mark of institutionalism. The result will be, of course, peaceful co-existence, which is a great good. But mere peaceful co-existence will also signify an end to development. Fine agreements, necessary though they may be, are not enough.

How many Churchmen envisage only an eschatological ecumenism—for the future life—as if visible unity were not to be realised here on earth. When the sense of compelling urgency is lost, we only go on prolonging indefinitely a situation in which each wants no more than to be heard by another.

Dialogue is indispensable in the search for unity, but on condition that it does not rest content with a static denominational truce. In face of the immense hopes which are being raised, the temptation arises to go on expounding endlessly the subtleties of denominational differences. Denominationalism is a self-defensive attitude. It could be justified in the past, but it dooms those who pursue it today to remain shut up within themselves. Moreover, denominational mentalities persist even when faith has disappeared. We all know Catholics or Protestants who only admit to a vague deism, but who maintain emotional hostilities when faced with a Christian of the other side.

There is one force which can enable us to go beyond our denominational positions; that is the challenge of those baptised millions who are living without adherence to God and of those multitudes who are totally indifferent to the faith.

The strongest resistance to all communication, all dialogue with them, is, in fact, within ourselves. Being open to everyone means to let our self-centredness be overcome, so that the Other than ourselves can penetrate into the depths of our being.

Ways open to us

In this age of ecumenism, paths of hope are opening up. In face of the gloomy prospects which the future presents, it is important to recall that quite often, in the most difficult times, a small number of men and women, scattered throughout the world, have been able to reverse the course of historical development because they hoped against all hope. What had been set for disintegration was then drawn into the current of a new dynamism.

In order that we may advance towards reconciliation, God gives us the means of freeing ourselves from ourselves. Through the great events of this century, we have the opportunity to break loose from the self-absorbing process which has kept Christianity bogged down for several centuries.

There are, among others, three truly ecumenical actions which can become events of God, ways of unity, and means of giving an entirely new dimension to the ecumenical movement:

(1) Avoiding the split between generations
(2) Meeting those who cannot believe
(3) Identifying ourselves with the poor of the world.

Certainly there are some refusals which will always raise up father against son, Christian against his separated brother. There will always be separations, there will always be fanatics only concerned with their own well being.

But if only all men committed to the same journey could now go forward together! And if only these united Christians could simply live without passing judgment on those who are travelling by other paths than theirs! For it is essential to see every man in the light of pure intentions, even those who are desperately defending an outdated attitude.

The Power of the Provisional

Back to the sources of the contemplative life

Marked by just such a missionary impulse, the new generations, in their generosity of spirit, want to go out to encounter all the current movements. In their search for a new power of communication, a means of reaching out to contemporary man, they are attempting to free themselves from the formulas and expressions of the past. How often do we hear their ardent appeal to demythologise, to "desacralise" all the expressions of our communication with God.

We are emerging from a long period in which formulations, symbols and signs in the life and prayer of the Church have been little understood. Hence the desire to make a clean sweep in order to approach God by other paths. This tendency may represent a healthy reaction against all that is purely automatic, against lack of participation, and stereotyped words.

Today we are coming to a new dawn. But in this new light we can still see that our relationship with God does not do away with the mystery. Quite the opposite: there still exists a line of demarcation which no one can cross, and beyond which the mystery remains.

In our desire to explain everything, we run the risk of no longer understanding anything at all; for it is true that the intellect alone is incapable of grasping the mystery of the Church. In order to penetrate the mystery, there is nothing more essential than actions and gestures, humble signs which reach to the depths of our person, the "archetypes" as some would call them today.

Religious fervour cannot be nourished simply by explanation. In the life of prayer in common, even those liturgical actions that are most completely explained are not strong enough to break down our automatic attitudes.

By reducing everything to a formula, we risk losing the sense of God. Thus a void is created into which can flow indifference or even refusal, since rebellion lies half-formed in every man and woman. The man who loses the sense of what is sacred is tempted to treat it with irony and to distort it into caricature. An underlying force within him strains to block any step towards humility, holding him back from bending the knee before the mystery of God and of the Church.

A man who wishes to identify himself with an increasingly secularised world, without losing in himself the sense of the sacred, must pursue a double action which will bring him ever closer to the sources of contemplative life.

(1) Live the mystery of the Church
(2) Remain in contemplative waiting upon God.

Confronted by the vast questions which arise, some are tempted to flee to a restricted ecclesiastical environment or to seek refuge in a form of contemplation which cuts them off from other people and from the great contemporary movements. Rather they should hasten forward to meet their neighbour, since contemplation is always linked to present realities. Yet those who are concerned with the younger generations, preoccupied by dialogue with unbelievers, and anxious to bring human advancement to the very poor, must not flee from the old institutions. They should rather hasten to their aid in order to renew them, to make their unity possible, and stay with them in contemplative waiting upon God. Otherwise their efforts will soon flag or turn into bitterness.

AVOIDING THE SPLIT
BETWEEN GENERATIONS

Coming to terms with today

SOME men are old from their youth. Orientated towards
a recent or a distant past, they cannot come to terms
with the changes taking place around them. Far from
accepting these changes, they endure them, "they shoot
out the lips, they shake the head".[1]

This is true in all societies. So many Christians pass
a final judgment on the very young and in this way
aggravate the rift between the generations. To grow
old without contact with the rising generations is to be
condemned to vegetate.

Because contemporary history is seeing such revolu-
tionary changes, we have to respond with an openness
of heart and mind not demanded of any previous generation if we want to grasp the great trends of the present
day. Knowledge acquired in youth will be increasingly
disproportionate to the level of present knowledge. But
the daily use of our intelligence gives us the opportunity
for constant rejuvenation, an adaptation to new situations.

As a man grows older, his thoughts are enriched, his judgment becomes finer, the accumulation of experience and knowledge give sharpness to his reflection which has no substitute: nothing can replace a life filled with years of hard work. The more a man is linked with eternity, and the more he knows what he is approaching, the better prepared he is to live. To grow old, then, is to have our youth renewed by everything that contemporary evolution brings us.

The older generation should not make decisions with reference to themselves alone, but neither must the younger generation be concerned only with the interests of their own age group. The Church is not a copy of secular societies. Within its framework everyone is committed together. The split between the generations is a contradiction of the meaning of ecumenism, and we all have everything to lose by it: the young because they no longer have the opportunity to benefit from the human and spiritual experience of their elders; the less young and the older because they are relegated to a situation where, no longer able to live, they must wait passively for their own death.

Today's generation is a hinge between two worlds; one in which ancestral and historical influences predominate, and the other which turns its back on these. Those who belong to this generation must refuse to be a generation sacrificed. On the contrary, they must be stimulated by the obligation to go forward and draw together the attitudes of the past and those of tomorrow.

Ecumenism involves everybody; it is very simply a welcome to everyone. It helps us to understand what is most pure in the aspirations of each person. To allow oneself to be isolated is contrary to the ecumenical venture, which always binds together, without ever breaking.

The thirst for fulfilment

As I have written these pages day by day, I have been kept alert, here in Taizé, by conversations with many different kinds of young people. They all have something in common—a great missionary impulse which drives them to enter into the tomorrow of mankind by taking part in bringing the institutions of the Church and the formulations of the faith up to date.

Denominationalism evokes a negative reaction among the younger generations, who reject all reference to a history which no longer relates to the present. They will tend more and more to gather together into autonomous groups. In contrast to their elders, these young generations will no longer have any time for denominational self-justification. They will go where life can be found. They are moulded by technological disciplines and a thirst for practical achievements; therefore they will not endure for long the evasions of the old institutions. If we do not offer them in the near future a Church United, which in our faith we confess as the only place for united brotherhood of all men, then they will search elsewhere and will turn to universalist ideologies or to a spiritual atheism.

Conscious of their own dynamism, they demand something genuine. They are apprehensive about an abstract ecumenism which would only be one more idea, an ideology. They would not support an ecumenism which only served as a smokescreen to disguise the malaise of separation. The hour has come for humble, but definite action.

Among the younger generation, there are two tendencies which are both animated by the same missionary impulse.

Some young people, distressed by the weight of institutions, translate their anxiety into aggression. They would choose to break up the structure and destroy the old fabric of Christian institutions. Their views on what has to be reconstructed in its place are sometimes purely theoretical.

Other young people are ready to consider concrete situations, and want to insert a new today into the life of the Church. They know that *"aggiornamento"* is not a game, a questioning for the pleasure of disturbing other people, a vicious circle inside which others are enclosed in order to satisfy a need for change. Consequently, they do not think of building in the abstract or in isolation.

True, several centuries of immobility weigh heavily on the situation which has to be overcome in the next decades: at any given moment, in order to hold fast, each Christian had to establish his own traditions even at the risk of cutting himself off from others. Immobility has made these structures even more unyielding, and has led inevitably to a process of disintegration: the man who no longer builds sooner or later destroys himself.

The urgency of the times requires us to call on those of our own denominational family to abandon a conformism which is rooted in the past. Now that the miracle of unity seems possible as we prepare together to rediscover a wholly new ardour, who could accept that great sections of God's Church should be torn down, either by a new hardening into immobility or by a destructive violence with no future?

Rediscovering the Gospel

The younger generation are demanding new signs. Should the Holy Spirit only speak through men of maturity, the wise men that we have perhaps become? Should He not also speak to the Church of God through the new generations? Do not their questions delve into the depths of our conscience?

This generation sometimes makes final judgments on men of the Church. It considers adults to have acquired excessive security, the privileges of institutions, and for this reason refuses all communication with them. It wants a Christian community without compromise. It is repelled by cleverness. It demands a new style, and when it does not find this, it would prefer to abandon the Church and to go where there seems to be a greater simplicity and a greater transparency in human relationships. In the past, schisms were the threat. Today, it is the indifference of the young.

What is this new generation saying to us? "Give us the living proof that you believe in God, that your trust is really in Him. Show us that you are living the Gospel in its original freshness, in a spirit of poverty, in solidarity with everyone, not only with the family of your own denomination."

The freshness of the Gospel? It is waiting upon God. It is living the dynamics of today. It is a constant return to the source. It is reconciliation.

To recover this original freshness of the Gospel, would we accept a second conversion? This is a poor phrase, charged with the emotivity sometimes accorded it by our forebears. But we adults, would we shrink from making readjustments which are all the more difficult because habits acquired over the years and pride of life are opposed to the spirit of poverty and expectant waiting on God? Pride of life creates a rift which drains away all the spiritual freshness of the Gospel. But if we accept this conversion in its totality, Christ will reach deep into our intelligence and our heart. He will enter our flesh to our very bowels, in such a way that we in our turn will have "bowels of mercy".[2]

Common creation

Whether they be Catholic or Protestant, the rising generations call for reform of the institutions which have grown old. Very often, however, they put the cart before the horse by forgetting that there can be no reform of the Church without reform of the individual. It is important that "being" should come before "doing". Every process of bringing up to date begins with the conversion of the person to Christ, the Lord of the Church and of its institutions. Obsessed with the desire for reform, we run the risk of forgetting that up-dating has its beginnings in the depths of our being.

To these young people I often say: In the brotherly unity which brings two generations together at Taizé today, we want to listen to the Holy Spirit in you, and so enlarge our minds, our spirits and our hearts. Pray to the Lord of the Church for our conversion, and we will build together and together we will say, "Look, Lord, upon your Church; consider mankind, our brothers throughout the world. We have become separated, we no longer succeed in coming together to build your Church. Break our self-sufficiency. Kindle in us all the fire of your love."

And again I say to them: If a thorough analysis of the institutions leads you to allow the great fabric of God's Church to collapse, your plans, however generous they may be, will be without a future. The life of the Church places us within the cloud of witnesses. No one builds from nothing. The power you feel pulsing within you can persuade you that you alone are going to build everything anew. But the genius of the Church is to construct with the help of all its members; do not sign its death warrant. Do not forget yesterday. Nothing lasting is accomplished without a common creation.

In the great community of the Church, as in every Christian community, whether of marriage or otherwise, each member, day after day, shares in the re-creation of the whole body. If one member is dominated by an individual impulse to create and accomplishes his work without integrating it into the common creation, he unknowingly destroys. The common life exists only

22

when all who partake in it share the single aim of building together. The sign of unity which will then shine out among men is more important than the noblest work done on the fringe of the community.

Our creation becomes a common creation when we consider what God is preparing for us. So many signs have been given to us today. God is preparing for us a Church restored in its unity, which will offer to the insecurity of men throughout the world a firm foundation for all. Violence is not necessary to achieve this unity. No one will be torn away from the family of his Church or his home. To act in this way would not be creation in common. It would be to wound love, and he who wounds love does not build the Church of God.

MEETING THOSE WHO
CANNOT BELIEVE

Ecumenism a prerequisite

WE Christians, living in the twentieth century, find ourselves confronted with the consequence of our divisions: a mutual impoverishment. Around us live the indifferent masses of the baptised or the unbaptised. They do not share our faith, they only believe in what they see. How can they take us seriously as long as our brotherly love is not a visible reality?

The time of confrontation is drawing near. This concerns us all, for it challenges all of us. After twenty centuries of Christianity, more and more of the baptised are becoming indifferent to the faith. Moreover, despite our Christian presence throughout the world, the human condition goes on deteriorating year by year in certain areas of this world.

Our unity concerns all these people. It exists for all of them. We do not pursue it in order to be more comfortable together, nor to be stronger against other people. We pursue it in order rightly to assume our missionary vocation. Such is the purpose of ecumenism: it is a prerequisite to the pastoral care of the masses.

We will never go out to meet those who do not believe, unless we are together. Not that we must turn our backs on the truth. But, when we agree on a fundamental truth, the necessity for visible unity, we discover the possibility of one day coming to agreement over the other truths of the faith.

A new dynamism is promised to those who find each other again after having been separated. Reconciliation brings with it an openness of spirit and of heart to every man, and even in advanced age he becomes young again. Reconciled with himself and his neighbour, he recovers a living power. In the same way, the old branches of Christianity, scattered across the world, will come to know, in the rediscovery of their visible unity a youth, a vigour and a new springtime.

There is a dynamism in reconciliation which will lead us out of the state of impoverishment caused by our divisions. This impetus will make it possible for us to overcome our inability to make contact with the world which, even if it does not expect much from us, would be right in expecting everything from men and women who bear the name of Christians.

But the confrontation, which is now in the making, will mean a total reawakening in the strongest sense of the word. If we are to go forward together to meet those who cannot believe, then we must daily make the hidden offering of our lives.

The true history of the ecumenical movement will never be written. It is found in the small and the great fidelities of those who take up the struggle in the very depths of their innermost being. For a long time yet, ecumenism will be moving against the current of conformity: dialogue with those most distant from us will never occur of its own accord. Whoever is not prepared to see this struggle through might well ask if his ecumenism is a plant without roots.

Dialogue with all men

At Taizé, our ecumenical vocation has made us more open, year by year, to all that is human. This calling has aroused our interest in those who were furthest from us. Without an ardent fervour for the unity of the Body of Christ, we should never have discovered this dimension of friendship for so many men throughout the world.

The concern for dialogue has made us aware of everything that is human. Who would not be consumed with a desire to understand his fellow-being in the struggle of his existence: to see in his expression either an extinguished flame, or a serenity achieved through self-conquest; to see in him either an attitude of recollection drawing together his whole being, or the scars of contradictory impulses, either the generous gift of himself or the ardent desire to withhold himself?

The spirit of mercy disposes a heart of stone to be transformed into a heart of flesh. It makes room for a strong charity and excludes all sentimentality which is a caricature of true feeling. It refuses to dramatise the subjective elements of a situation. And it welcomes with quiet confidence whoever, and whatever, it may meet.

How does it happen that so many Christians, while claiming to know God, live as if they had never found Him, and remain without mercy? They use the name of the God of Jesus Christ and yet their hearts stay hardened.

On the other hand, how does it happen that so many agnostics, together with the publicans and sinners "go before us into the Kingdom", open up for us a way of peace, are men of reconciliation and show a deeper concern than many Christians for peaceful relations between all men?

It is possible to believe that such men, without professing an explicit faith, carry Christ within them without knowing it. May it not be that the prayers of countless Christians throughout the ages are achieving this very result? Men are hearing God without knowing Him, they are obeying Him and live in a creative love. Must we not apply Christ's words to them: "they go before us into the Kingdom of God"?[3] They open the gates and mark out the way.

Many are those who profess to love Christ but know Him not. Many are those who love Him while claiming not to know Him. Many are those who are children of light without knowing it. Yet it is easy to recognise them: in their concern for their neighbour, they flee the works of darkness, and all that brings obscurity and confusion. It is up to us to understand them and help them to realise explicitly what God has entrusted to them. To go beyond oneself, and to do overt acts of charity, are already signs of Christ, signs of an implicit faith.

Dialogue with the man who does not believe makes it possible for us to reveal in him what he does not know of himself, the mystery of a hidden presence. To be able to discern the image of God in every man, this is the mark of true dialogue. A Christian who senses in his neighbour truly ecumenical values, and who seeks in him the man whom God created, can benefit from the mutual re-creation which is part of all dialogue.

It goes without saying that only the man who at every moment renews himself in the Word of God, in the Eucharist and in a firm devotion can truly speak in this way. Otherwise he would fall into a relativism which benefits no one. To say that some people, without knowing God, follow Him unwittingly, could be taken as an invitation not to strive for Christ any longer: what further use is it to pray, to be in God's presence and to meditate?

If generosity is not built upon a firm foundation, it is laid open to atrophy or spiritual slackness. Only the man who lives in the peace of Christ, rooted and grounded in the living Word, can recognise the image of Christ in those who profess no faith.

IDENTIFYING OURSELVES WITH THE POOR OF THE WORLD

Poverty without charity, shadow without light

POVERTY is a word that skins one's lips. In writing the Rule of Taizé I hardly dared use it; it flowed uneasily from my pen. Thinking that the spirit of poverty was primarily in simple and generous sharing, I preferred to speak of the commitment to the community of goods "to the extent of visible poverty".

Often a puritanical attitude prevails which consists in making things seem poor, that is seem dull, while actual resources are hidden behind a washed-out façade. If the spirit of poverty becomes synonymous with gloom and austerity, is it really in keeping with the first Beatitude? The spirit of poverty is in the joy of a man whose security lies in God. It shows itself in the outward signs of joy.

How can we ignore the reaction of workers who resent this language in the Gospel? They think that by idealising poverty Christians wish to keep the working classes in a state of inferiority, in subjection to the leisured classes. We must try to understand the desire for social and human improvement that motivates these men.

The expression, "The Church of the Poor", has become popular with many nowadays. It can have an impact and reawaken consciousness of a demand of the Gospel. We can rejoice in so far as it is a protest against the serious worldly compromises which weigh down our Christian world. None the less, this expression can only have an educational and purely provisional value: the Church is for everyone, even if the poor have a privileged place in it.

An increasingly strong call to poverty is making itself felt among Christians. The younger generations are very hard on any suggestion of luxury. The strong criticism made by many young laymen springs from the right motives, but if we accept renunciation we must recognise that it is not restricted to material things. The fact of having limited means might lead us, without our knowing it, to look for a different form of security, for example by imposing ourselves on the minds of others, and forcing them to enter into our own way of seeing things. The spirit of poverty embraces the whole of our being. Outward signs of poverty are not enough; they still leave room for human ambition, the urge for power, and the desire to dominate one's neighbour, which outward appearances only disguise.

To put forward an ideal which is unattainable in an

31

affluent society means that those who seek a life of poverty according to the Gospel are forced to live in a situation of continual tension; they want to attain the inaccessible. The aim of the Gospel is not to destroy personality, it is only trying to arouse a healthy discontent. To demand the impossible leads to critical situations. There are some demands which keep us locked up in inner conflicts. Are we not witnessing in certain cases the establisment of a new kind of Jansenism?

The vow of poverty itself, if it is aggressively asserted, not only enlightens no one but is destructive on account of the bitterness which it contains. A man or woman who has taken the vow of poverty must never forget the father and mother of a family who have children to care for. The demands of our life cannot be theirs. They can so easily become oppressive for them and prevent them from understanding our vows. Aggressive poverty arouses fear.

The spirit of poverty must not become hard; it must not become judging. We must not exalt one Beatitude at the expense of others. The poor man is gentle, he is the poor man of Yahweh, dependent at every moment on God alone.

In this sphere it is essential to maintain a just balance. Poverty is nothing without charity, a shadow without light. He who, in the name of poverty, makes a complacent condemnation of his neighbour, can be certain that he is in the wrong.

The first Beatitude in action

The spirit of poverty constantly needs putting into action. In the northern hemisphere economic growth and human progress are going on all the time. Consequently there are ways of being present in the world of the poor which very soon become outdated and obsolete.

On the other hand, the existence of the world of the poor in the southern hemisphere could be seen by Christians in the West as an act of God, which could help them not to shut themselves up in their affluent societies, and enable them to escape from that turning in on themselves which is characteristic of all old societies.

This is why it is important, as an ecumenical action, to make fresh contact with the world of the poor and to link ourselves with it. Otherwise, because of the growth of population which every day is becoming more marked in the southern hemisphere, the meeting of the two worlds could well be transformed into an apocalyptic conflict.

In this period of great tensions *"aggiornamento"*, bringing up to date, is indispensable. Much more than a superficial bringing up to date, what is needed is a spiritual attitude which demands the most fundamental reforms on the level of human thought and commitment. The poor of Christ will help us to make these changes. Their very existence calls us to transform our attitudes. Through our contact with them we are able to take a step back and look at ourselves. It is with them that we shall undergo a reconversion, otherwise we run the risk of producing a Christian society in the West which is advancing too fast and is enclosed in the vicious circle of merely human achievements.

In order to carry out our *"aggiornamento"* with the poor, we must all of us, Christians of different denominations, put the first Beatitude into action in two stages:

(1) Rediscovering, by contact with them, *the spirit of poverty*. Receiving instead of giving, whether we stay where we are or go where they live. Rediscovering the sense of God's Providence.

(2) Making a fresh search for *a social doctrine of ecumenism*; finding a common denominator so that we can go together to meet the world of the poor.

Surely it is not too much to say that one of the strongest impulses of ecumenism will come from the world of the poor.

Living the spirit of poverty

In the Israel of God there existed a community of the poor of Yahweh. They stood before God, stripped of everything, looking for the coming of the Messiah. Their whole existence was turned towards the imminent fulfilment of the promise. To have heaped up possessions would have given the lie to their hopes. The Virgin Mary was a member of this community. Free and waiting on her Lord, she could say yes with a faithful heart.

Amongst the underprivileged who are suffering in the world today, many belong to the community of Christ's poor. With a greater or lesser intensity they live in expectation of His return. The man who is prepared to identify himself with them will find one of the greatest treasures in the Gospel among them, the sense of God's providence, which Christians of the West have lost, having been weakened by the speed of social evolution. In contact with the poor, we rediscover the sense of urgency, but at the same time the power of expectation, and through them we become capable of understanding what our dull spirits were no longer able to grasp.

To have the soul of a poor man, to realise that one is completely poor, is to be weak with those who are weak, prepared to be assisted oneself in times of disaster. The weakness of any one person, even in the furthest corner of the world, is my weakness also. When someone is about to fall—in my own Church family or in another denomination—how can I not go to his assistance? For too long we have believed that mutual aid should be confined to those of our own denomination, to the stage where we remained indifferent to the weakness of anyone in another denomination who was about to stumble.

The spirit of poverty calls for simplicity in the use of material possessions. This makes us freer in our relationship with God. Accept with simplicity what is given you today, without ever yielding to the temptation of storing up reserves. In the desert, the people of Israel tried to keep the manna from heaven until the next day, but already it was rotting.

Inspired by a spirit of poverty, man depends on God alone. Poor in talents, poor in means; but He is there, He who will heap riches upon us. Accumulating securities of every kind gives the lie to our confidence. To abandon them is to be in search of God, and to have no unshakable security except in Him.

In general, in our affluent environment, is it possible to put the first Beatitude into practice in any other way than by a straightforward use of material things while always continuing in search of God? It is true that many men and women who have made the vow of poverty hear a more radical challenge. As their poverty involves making no judgment on others, its meaning is clear to laymen: it is a joyful waiting for the return of Christ and a genuine solidarity with all those, throughout the world, who do not have their daily bread. It is also the protest of the Christian conscience against those who abuse the good things of the earth. The earth is given to man for him to use. It is his way to freedom, never, never a means of destroying the freedom of others.

Towards a social doctrine of ecumenism

The danger for ecumenism is that it will get bogged down in the predicaments of Western Christendom. For anyone who knows how many struggles for power have been fought out in the past in our Christian societies, and how many struggles are going on at present in spite of some improvement in the situation, the question must be this: will not the field of action which will free us from our present attitudes and show us the way to reconciliation be discovered far beyond the limits of our own concerns?

At present, two thirds of mankind suffer from hunger. We, who are in danger of becoming indifferent, or even cynical and spiritually dull, on account of having enough and more than enough, must ask ourselves whether we are prepared to share the material and spiritual benefits which are showered upon us. Do we realise that in Latin America women and children are sometimes reduced to living standards which we would not even accept for our domestic animals? Are we going to take part in the tremendous efforts which this demands of Christendom?

We are confronted with Christ's poor to whom our blunted consciences have remained indifferent. We are required to go and meet them, and in order to do this we must all search together for a social doctrine of ecumenism. The chapter headings will be: sharing, working together, meeting together, participating in the advancement of mankind.

Today, more is required of us than generosity and detachment. Communion with those who suffer in the world means participation in the struggle against that suffering. Those who want to go to underdeveloped countries need a technical training. Goodwill is not enough. The possibilities are cruelly limited. What is expected from us is above all to take part in this human advancement while remaining where we are, and to make it possible for young people of the underdeveloped countries to receive training, ideally in their own countries, where they themselves can promote the development of their own people.

Many historical developments would be reversed if

Christians alone could even now make the words of Peter true and say: "Silver and gold have I none",[4] nothing stored up, nothing left over. That in itself would be enough to establish truer justice on earth. The younger generations steer clear of us Christians when we talk cheerfully of security in God while often needing the reassurance of gold and silver.

Brotherly community cannot exist without visibly sharing possessions. An intolerable schism will one day overthrow the whole equilibrium of the West, if we do not extend our concern to the two thousand million people whose poverty is continually increasing, and if we do not attempt to share our bread with them by actions which will be humble but effective.

To share bread is one of the realities of the Gospel, but we dread depriving ourselves of our securities. However, those who have set out on this road can bear witness that bread has always been given them. By sharing, our prayer for daily bread becomes real, and we enter into the sense of the provisional, and the child-like spirit of the Beatitudes.

If we put such a social doctrine into action, we hold a powerful weapon for ecumenism in our hands. In one and the same action, the separated Christians of the West will be brought together in close co-operation and will be linked with the poor of the southern hemisphere.

39

In joining together to bring material improvement to those who could no longer hope for it, we shall have returned to the universal vocation of the baptised. The past will be left far behind, with out blind struggles for power, our unacknowledged craving to be right in face of everyone else. In return, those with whom we have shared our bread, will return to us a hundredfold what we have tried to give them: they will give us our visible unity, rediscovered by working together with one another and with them.

LIVING THE MYSTERY OF
THE CHURCH

Accepting the institutions of the Church

THE institution is the environment where, generally, we find ourselves placed by our birth. Sometimes it is a heavy handicap in our relationship with Christ and the Church; it seems to load us with an almost unbearable weight, and almost stifle in us the evangelical exuberance which is the mark of the Christian. Some sort of reconversion or rebaptism seems desirable.

But little by little, through the gradual working out of the life of Christ in us, and by an undramatic progress, we discover that the spiritual life of each Christian is precisely what gives new life to the institutions to assure continuity and hand on the faith, but they would be nothing without the inner life of individual men and women who, "having been grasped by Christ, wish in their turn to grasp Him".[5] Such is our first relationship with the institutions that carry the weight of centuries: our commitment to Christ inspires and gives them new life.

Without returning to the sources of the faith no

reconciliation is possible, nor any effort to make contact with a world which cannot believe. Only the man who is firmly rooted in the mystery of the Church is capable of going out to meet all men.

Because of their origin, the Eastern Churches are a great help to us in this respect. They put more emphasis on mystical values, which balances the accent which the West puts on speculative theology. In this way they lead us to contemplate the mysteries of the faith; this, more than explanation, allows us to worship the presence of the Holy Spirit, and to understand what the Communion of Saints means. And in their liturgy something of the invisible shines through, that invisible which to a greater or lesser extent is what all men, believers or non-believers, long for.

When we consider the mystery of the Church, when we fully accept our solidarity with all the baptised, without our knowing it a purification takes place within us and the Lord works in us.

By accepting the institutions of the Church, by making ourselves one with them, we become much more capable of being the leaven in the lump. When yeast is a real leaven, what a power it has to swell the dough and to burst through the crust which always forms on ageing institutions! Nothing resists such a leaven.

It may be necessary to react against the dead weight of an ecclesiastical body in order to renew what is decrepit in it. But if those who express this reaction become agitators and if, moreover, they organise themselves and protest from outside, they prevent the advance of institutions wearied by a long struggle, and hinder their reform. One does not reform a body, however small, by the threat of schism. It is always from within and with infinite care that one brings new life where it is needed. Only then is confrontation constructive. Every schism which, at the time, seems to relieve tension, is in reality an impoverishment. It means a refusal to take the further steps which are essential to a life in God which will be fully responsible and united.

Certainly for some people the temptation to withdraw and form a small group of the élite is very great. But it must be realised that, under the pressures of history, "small remnants" risk becoming hardened and no longer life-bearing. And everything that does not advance life is destined to die. The variety of spiritual families in the Church is an element of health and unity. But those whose idiosyncrasies can only survive at the price of separation, are the opponents of unity.

By revering the mystery of the Church, by accepting our limitations in the face of certain burdens, we become able, when it is necessary and when the time is ripe, to demand, to beg, to beseech; in this way the event bursts forth from the heart of the old institutions without shattering its unity.

The man who would be content, in his personal life or that of the Church, to look only for the event of God, and would thus place himself only in the perspective of what is provisional, would see his expectation brought to nothing. By not accepting that the action of God is woven into history, and into the continuity of tradition, he runs the risk of being like a pearl cast before swine.

On the other hand, an institution which refuses to consider the event of God as something always possible forgets the value of expectation, and deprives itself of the power of the provisional; it condemns itself to becoming rigid and loses its power to communicate. To maintain stereotyped forms in the name of tradition is to caricature tradition itself, that great current which flows through the ages and the life of the Church, carrying with it and within it essential values and the living Word of God. The man who no longer expects anything becomes static, and deprives himself of all power to communicate.

There can be great tension and even much suffering, at the moment when the event of God bursts through the institution. At this moment the contemplation of Christ and of the mystery of the Church comes, more than ever before, to the help of our impatience, restoring us to serenity.

Authority, an element of unity

Among the various institutions of the Church, authority is being more and more called into question. This rejection goes along with a mentality which has no further use for parental influence. The function of authority in the Church is to create unity. Authority exists to gather together and reunite those who are always becoming separated, divided, antagonistic to one another. He who is given authority is first of all a servant. His pastoral task, his service, is to help the Christian community entrusted to him to move towards unanimity, that is to say literally to have one soul, *"una anima"*. The Church is a structured society, but above all it is a brotherly one.

A Christian community which is a visible image of unity needs a leader to fulfil its purpose, a man who is given the task of reuniting, encouraging when necessary, and above all of reminding everyone of the spirit of mercy without which no Christian community can exist. If the Church demands at the head of each community a man who encourages unanimity, who gathers together those who always drift apart, should she not also accept a shepherd of the shepherds and of the various communities, who will work tirelessly to bring them together?

Many refuse all authority, maintaining that the dignitaries of the Church, more than any others, give way to ambition. It is true that pride and vanity threaten men of the Church. Ambition is totally opposed to poverty of spirit. As it grasps more and more ground, so its hunger grows greater. It always needs new pastures. The trends of contemporary psychology create in many people a desire for "self-fulfilment". Many chase after the mirage of the ambition to "fulfil themselves". But what does self-fulfilment mean in the language of the Gospel? Humility is certainly one of the great struggles one has with oneself, especially in a man who takes on authority. The gratification of pride brings a momentary peace, but the need for more power comes back, always more imperious.

At the centre of the government of the Churches and Christian communities, those who hold authority sometimes yield to these same inner processes of authoritarianism and cleverness, and succumb to the injuries of humiliation which, in order to be healed, seek compensation in further ambition.

Ecclesiastical structures which are not hierarchical do not preserve those in positions of responsibility from these dangers and put them in a privileged situation. Pastors become the victims of an inhuman, ecclesiastical power. Authoritarianism worms its way in everywhere, among the leaders of the Protestant Churches as elsewhere. Certain of them probably need that very power which they sometimes condemn in those who belong to hierarchical institutions.

Nevertheless it is important, while profiting from this valuable concept of authority in the Gospel, to understand those who, saddled with the responsibilities of the Church, sometimes no longer succeed in finding the necessary time to come face to face with God. According to all the evidence, Churchmen like these, overloaded with work, think that the first essential is to carry out their most immediate duties. Lack of time sometimes make them give up dialogue with God. The overdevelopment of activities no longer allows them time for the vital withdrawal into God.

A profound understanding of these human situations is a way which helps us live the mystery of the Church.

Solidarity with all who are baptised

The ecumenical vocation leads us inescapably to reflect on the mystery of the Church, since a faith which is not fully thought out is condemned to waste away. It is threatened with sentimentality and is in danger of being unable to communicate itself.

One of the themes on which we must meditate is the way in which all Christians, through their baptism, belong to Christ and His mystical body. Orthodox, Catholic, Protestant, we are marked with a universal seal by the same baptism, chosen to become men who can discern in every creature the very image of the Creator.

We all confess our relation to Christ, the head, and to the Church, his body, in the same words of the creed. When we declare "I believe in the Communion of Saints", we affirm: I believe that between the departed witnesses and the Christians alive today, between the Church Triumphant and the Church Militant which fights and prays, there exists a relationship which nothing can destroy. The very same communion binds together all the baptised living in the world today. Because of this common baptism, by which we are rooted in Christ, we are called to live in solidarity with all those baptised and to hold fast an unshakable brotherhood.

For a Catholic, being in solidarity with all the baptised signifies first of all being in solidarity, inside his own Church, with all the spiritual families which make up Catholicism. In this period of history, what we expect of Catholics is that they should not deny one another. If the different trends which are becoming evident prevent dialogue, this would be an unparallelled setback for ecumenism.

At the core of their confusion, those with a sense of continuity, a sense of the sacred, need to recognise that those opposite them are people above all concerned with dialogue with men far from the faith. Those who have been given a sense of the mystery of the Church should not keep the irreplaceable worth of what they possess to themselves, but should try to understand those whose firm concern is for dialogue with contemporary man. At the same time those Catholics who are constantly on the alert in their advanced positions, should understand that without a daily return to the sources they will very soon have nothing to offer but emptiness.

After an initial period of inevitable tension, we await the time when the different spiritual families will discover in each other the best of what each has to offer and their evangelical values.

For a Protestant, to be in solidarity with the baptised means first of all being in solidarity with all the movements which exist in Protestantism. It is easy enough to accuse a Baptist, a Pentecostal, in whom we see no reflection of ourselves, of being sectarian. Nevertheless their position is a result of the Reformation and therefore solidarity is called for.

At Taizé, we try to live this solidarity with the whole of Protestantism. We consider ourselves to be united not with one confessional family alone, but with all those denominations which make up Protestantism, whatever they may be. By first of all accepting this solidarity on the level of confessional families, we are able to identify ourselves with all those who have received baptism. This calls for goodwill and serenity. To remain in solidarity with all those who have been baptised demands a mastery of oneself which has to be renewed day by day. Generosity to those baptised in another denomination can never be a mistake.

This openness does not mean abandoning a position of faith. It is not opposed to real vigilance over those whom God has entrusted to us. It does not involve doctrinal relativism, but rather deeper commitment to the faith.

Nothing is more contrary to solidarity than a deceptive ecumenism, an ecumenism which takes no risks. Those who practise it show much goodwill and balanced judgment in dialogue with Christians of another denomination, but criticise them as soon as they are back among themselves. In this way, they win acclaim amongst those of their own Church, who support ecumenism on condition that everything remains as it has been in the past.

This deceiving attitude, not to say a two-faced way of living, towards ecumenism is one of the greatest temptations. It preludes a future of disappointment. To call oneself ecumenical, while being afraid of unity, could imprison the ecumenical movement within the institution; this would prevent it from moving forward.

But the task of the institution is to take up every ecumenical vocation.

Advance, not flight

In 1519, commenting on the text of scripture, "Bear ye one another's burdens, and so fulfil the law of Christ",[6] Luther seized the opportunity of expressing his views on the schism of the Hussites in Bohemia, which occurred before the Reformation:

> "The Bohemians who have separated themselves from the Church of Rome can well make excuses: but they are nothing short of unholy and opposed to all the commandments of Christ. In fact their separation is contrary to the love which sums up all the commandments. The strongest accusation against them is precisely what they advance as their sole defence: that they made the separation through fear of God and motivated by conscience, since it was wrong to live among corrupt priests and popes. But whether priests or popes or anyone else be corrupt, if you were burning with true Christian love, you would not flee from them but would run towards them, if need be from the end of the world, to weep, beg and persuade, and stir all into action.
>
> "Realise that, in obeying the teaching of the

In one sense, the vocation of the Reformation was, at the beginning, to be a corrective to Catholicism and a deepening of it. However, since then Protestantism has sometimes established itself in isolation which does not correspond to its original aim. A further attitude is liable to follow from this: simply to wait until the Catholic Church "protestantises" itself.

These positions, in the long run, have become hardened. What once was a conflict of conscience gave place to an attitude of self-justification or self-satisfaction, existing on both sides. Those who had not sought the schism gloried in their prerogative, while those who provoked it considered themselves on the right side of the fence: had they not pulled out the tares from the wheat?

Catholics and Protestants lock themselves up in defensive attitudes. In order to protect its members from further schisms, the Catholic Church initiated and encouraged the movement of the Counter-Reformation. In many respects its ideas developed in opposition to Protestantism. On the Protestant side, confessional systems were built up in a spirit of hostility to all that seemed Catholic. Furthermore the history of Protestantism has seen communities which, because of their smallness, were forced to justify their existence in the face of the Catholic majority. The self-defensive attitudes which this causes soon characterises a whole mentality.

If the institutions on both sides are reformed, that day will dawn when we cannot but join together. If the *"aggiornamento"* is mutual, then surely it must bring us together. It will harmonise the complementary elements stemming from the Reformation with those of the Catholic tradition.

Certainly even the best reforms will always be followed by some surviving elements of sectarianism. But this is no cause for discouragement.

On the Catholic side, the Council has opened a way. Here is a promise for the future of Christianity. A new dynamism has been revealed, an event of God has burst from the heart of the Catholic institution, to the extent of terrifying certain non-Catholics, who dread being swallowed up in a powerful movement. But when the first surprise is over, those non-Catholics who are most alert will come to appreciate this event which, far from destroying or shattering the institution, offers it new life.

We Protestants, for our part, must make up our minds, whether we are going to remain simply turned in on our own history, or whether we in our turn are going to bring about an *"aggiornamento"*, and put our reforms into practice.

After four and a half centuries, we must recognise the need to bring Protestantism up to date, to rediscover the dynamics of the provisional, which originally was the reason for its existence; not to set itself up to last for ever. It is true that this bringing up to date is made difficult when certain Catholics talk of "the return" of their separated brothers. This expression hurts because it suggests an unconditional surrender. Such an idea is far from the mentality of the man of today, who, as he hastens forward, is struggling to go beyond himself. The unity of Christians will not involve the triumph of one group over another. No one would accept a unity which involved the victory of some and the defeat of others.

We Protestants are in danger today of living in two illusions.

Children of a Reformation, we might think that the reforms have been made once and for all. We believed that we had rediscovered the purity of the Church's original impulse. But already it is difficult to agree about the moment when that first period of the early Church came to an end. Moreover, have not our own communities in their turn been injured by complacency, and by the accumulation of traditions, institutions, and doctrinal trends more and more separated from the original spirit of the Reformation? Our institutions are weighed down by more than four centuries. Who will dare to instigate new and profound reforms to make contact with contemporary man?

Another illusion would be to suppose that Catholicism

is going to "protestantise" itself through the reforms coming from the Council. This would be to hold on to an idea of "return" no different from that which we criticise in others. We should only have to stay where we are and wait till the Catholics come to us.

A God-given moment is offered us today. Can we take it in simplicity of heart and in humility? Are we going to retreat again into self-justification or can we advance to encourage, convince, sustain and carry through the reform of the Church of God?

Putting an end to the schism

The Christian struggle is already so demanding! Why exhaust oneself with condemnation? Why tire oneself out by despising tendencies different from one's own? Arguments which stem from blind hatred prove nothing. Only generous attempts to understand the behaviour of our separated brother give us the right to underline the things which separate us.

Many Christians, particularly those in minority groups, whatever their denominational allegiance, are still using anathemas, as though their only means of survival was always to be on the defensive. In their aggressiveness these men always claim that tendencies other than their own are not representative. But what do the men who speak this way represent? What influence have they on the world of today and the progress of the Church?

We are often hypersensitive about matters which concern our denominational standpoints. Did not our fathers bravely defend these very standpoints? To look back at these past struggles paralyses our energies. We soon pass beyond being sensitive. We become touchy, and to avoid being hurt, take refuge by withdrawing into ourselves. The only way out is to refuse to pay attention to past and present wounds.

The call to reconciliation and solidarity is a message which can reach everyone. Men in institutions have too easy a tendency to label as naïve the faith of those who want to give proof that things are really moving forward by actions which are unconventional. It is a serious matter to caricature the way in which the truly humble express their faith, and to confuse child-like spirit with one of childishness. To accuse those who, in the simplicity of their prayer, confidently expect everything from God, of naïvety and sentimentality, is to deny the commitment of their faith.

Take two married couples, both separated, but both looking for reconciliation. The concern of the first is with the past. They are not living the today of God. Each wishes to justify himself, to be given guarantees, and educate the other. Over and over again convincing reasons are produced, and arguments multiply. It is impossible for them to meet. The second has a kind of intuition: if the family is ever to find true reconciliation, the only solution is for them to come together under the same roof and try to live together. So there must be no recriminations, and we must abandon once and for all the self-righteousness of separation, in order to find each other again in a completely new solidarity.

Once the opening dialogue has taken place, Christian unity can only be achieved by an act of faith consisting in the visible manifestations of our solidarity, bringing us all together at the heart of the same ecclesial reality. Those who, though still separated, live in the expectation of unity, know that their situation is only provisional. This is what keeps them going. For those who are still in expectation, the price of Christian unity is this: to be always willing to go beyond one's present position towards the fullest realisation of ecumenism.

The Eucharist, at the same time the method and fulfilment of unity, is alone able to give us the supernatural power and strength needed to realise unity on earth between those who are baptised. In doing this, we discover a living truth. As a sacrament of unity, it is offered to us in order that in us and around us, all that makes for separation may be dissolved. In it, those who through mutual ignorance, despised one another, are brought together.

The ecumenical movement will come to a halt if the day does not come soon when all who believe in the real presence of Christ in the Eucharist, though of separate denominations, are reunited round the same table.

Woven into history

In establishing at Taizé a common life at the heart of Protestantism, we have no other intention than to bring together men who wish to commit themselves to follow in the footsteps of Christ, in order to be a living sign of the Church's unity.

Community life brings into being a microcosm of the Church; on a small scale it gives an image of the whole reality of the Church. Thus the humble sign of a community can have effects which far transcend the limitations of its members. Much more than ideas, the world of today needs images. No idea could possibly gain credit, unless supported by a visible reality; otherwise it would only be an ideology. The sign, however weak, gains value in that it is a living reality.

To be honest in our ecumenical vocation means that there is in our common life a real demand for unity. That we should be sixty men belonging to several different Protestant Churches has in no sense caused a separation amongst us. Little by little, unity of faith is created amongst us through our liturgical prayer. We know that we are not exempt from difficulties, because the struggle is fierce. But if we had to start again we should not hesitate.

Because of the immense freedom inherent in our situation, we need not have taken any notice of those who have preceded us in the common life. But what would this life have been, lived apart from all solidarity? Reverence for the mystery of the Church has come to help us see that Taizé is only a simple shoot grafted on to a great tree, without which it could not live.

From this point of view there is without doubt significance in the fact that our village is situated between Cluny and Cîteaux.

On one side is Cluny, the great Benedictine tradition which made human all that it touched. Cluny, with its sense of proportion, and of the visible community built up in unity. Cluny, the point of attraction for men who consciously or unconsciously were searching for unity within themselves, and with their neighbour.

Among the Abbots of Cluny we find that eminent Christian, Peter the Venerable, so human, so concerned with love and unity, capable of actions centuries in advance of his time. In the very name of unity, when two popes had been elected by the Conclave, he was generous enough to ask for the withdrawal of the man from Cluny, one of his sons. Overcoming the prejudices of his time, he welcomed and offered a place of retreat to Abelard when everyone else condemned him.

In this period of history, we again find him arousing men in words of fire by proclaiming to them the power which comes from meeting God face to face:

"Jesus will always be with me, and He will not turn aside from me at any time. Surely at every moment, scorning and rejecting all that is not Him, I will attach myself to Him alone. Jesus will be my life, my food, my rest, my joy. For me He will be homeland and glory. Jesus will be my all: as far as is possible here on earth through hope and love, until the threshold of eternity: then I will see Him face to face, He has promised it."[9]

On the other side there is Cîteaux, given new life in the time of Peter the Venerable by another Christian no less remarkable: St. Bernard.

St. Bernard anticipated all the reforming energy which was to explode in the sixteenth century. He renewed Cîteaux in order to reform the rule lived at Cluny. He refused in any way to compromise with the demands of the Gospel. He had the voice of a reformer, and more a sense of urgency than of the great continuities. To one of his brothers he wrote:

"There is nothing stable in this world . . . We must

necessarily either go forward or go back. It is impossible to be static. He who does not try to progress is already moving backwards. It is Jesus Christ who is the prize in this race. If you stop while He moves on with giant strides, not only will you fail to reach the prize, but the goal will become even more distant from you."[10]

It is absolutely vital to continue this sense of urgency, assured through many generations, in order to secure inner peace and humility: I am a useless servant; what I do not accomplish myself others will do after me. Others will be able to gather the ripened fruit from what is now unready.

Called to the same commitment, we are grateful to those who have preceded us for having remained steadfastly loyal to the great call of the Gospel: leaving everything and receiving on earth a hundredfold, with persecutions. They have given witness by their brotherly life, which has so often made people say, "See how they love one another", they have been obedient to God, shown by their humble faithfulness from day to day, by the continuity of their praise through the centuries, and by so many other qualities continued down the ages; by doing this they give us their support, they give us a cause for hope.

Across a great diversity of spiritual families, they have

kept the unity necessary for building up the body of Christ. Both in witnessing to unity, and in offering their lives afresh day by day, they guide us to the very footsteps of Christ.

Some have argued that at Taizé we have wanted to free the common life from the weight of its traditions. If this were the case, our existence would embody a judgment which, although implicit, would be none the less severe. By it we would be contradicting our very vocation, namely unity. We would be protesters, and by the same token, would shut ourselves up in an attitude of complacency. The road to unity is never through protest. If we made external judgments on others, we should simply shut ourselves up within ourselves.

When we are told of certain problems which weigh on this or that institution, we keep silent, since external judgments always result in making positions more rigid. When people are in trouble we should want to love them all the more. And if we are given the chance to express ourselves, we do so only when we are certain of not encouraging a spirit of revolt.

Now, at the great turning point of contemporary history, it is more urgent than ever to consider, all of us together, the essence of our common life, and make it the reality it ought to be. By its very nature, all life in community is turned towards God and towards men. If it only encouraged purity of living, it would be in great danger of dying a slow death. It requires a capacity for constant renewal. Those who live this life make proper use of the freedom given by their condition if they keep a step ahead of the world and of the Church. It is pointless being too far ahead, but falling behind would destroy the vitality of the committed life.

Community life, more so today than ever before, as long as it flows with the sap which is proper to it, as long as it replenishes itself with the freshness of the life of brotherhood which is its essence, becomes a powerful force, both in the Church and in the world, capable of moving mountains of indifference, and bringing to men the irreplaceable benefit of the presence of Christ.

LIVING IN CONTEMPLATIVE EXPECTATION OF GOD

Awaiting and provisional

OFTEN, gathered together with my brothers for common prayer in the Church, I have been astonished how these men, my companions in life, remain faithful in expectation of God. They stand before God without seeing, and in a sense without knowing, what responses their expectation will have. I marvel at the determination of these men, their dedication and the joy which prevails over the inner struggles.

It is very true that throughout the whole of our life as Christians, we live in expectation. Ever since Abraham, the first believer, and together with his seed, we live in expectation of God, of his justice and of the Event which comes from Him. But for the man who is no longer in expectation and is satisfied in himself, with his privileges and his rights, a whole dimension of faith becomes limited.

To know this is to know also that we are in a state which is always provisional, and "provisional" has the same root as "provide": to provide the necessary measures for the present, while awaiting another state of affairs.

What is peculiar to us at Taizé may perhaps one day have to disappear. Our liturgy leads us to a unanimity in faith and supports a strong hope. It makes us live, as on the evening of Emmaus, in the presence of the Risen One whom our eyes are kept from seeing. And yet, is not this a provisional state, which is destined to disappear on the day of visible unity?

The man who lives in the provisional sees his journey towards unity given a new impulse. The supreme threat would be for us to become self-sufficient, to close the lid on the newly discovered treasure and then to institute, for centuries to come, structures which, once outmoded, become factors of isolation and not of communication. All available strength would go into making the structures last.

Do we not see in the history of Christians so many institutions which lost the provisional character with which they began, in order to survive the passage of time? The Christian horizon of those who belong to these institutions is contracted. They survive only by withdrawing behind walls that offer them protection.

There is no reconciliation without mutual renunciation. On the day of visible unity, it will still be necessary to die to a part of ourselves. Unless the grain dies, can it bear fruit?

What must die, of course, is what is peculiar to the family, and not what is common to all. As with Christian married couples, we are held to a fidelity and changelessness of vocation, especially as concerns our vows and promises. They cannot be held in question, for they not only provide the means of our commitment to follow Christ, but also the framework at whose heart we have been reunited in the same family.

It must be stressed that only he who has the sense of continuity can benefit from the dynamics of the provisional. Enthusiasm, meaning fervour, is a positive force; but it is not enough. As a force, it becomes exhausted and dies away if it can no longer communicate its impetus to some other force, more deeply buried and less sensitive, which sustains us during our life. Continuity must be maintained, because our enthusiasms are interspersed with times of monotony and with arid wastes. It is one of life's laws: intermittent periods of rest and of emptiness are all part of going forward.

Prayer must therefore be regular. To complain about this much-needed fidelity, would be, in fact, to complain about oneself. For when the time comes, this regularity and continuity will act as a support to win back the impulse. The one depends on the other: enthusiasm as a feature of the provisional and continuity as a feature of hope.

Hold on in serenity

The ecumenical vocation is unquestionably an ordeal by fire, a struggle which requires complete mastery of oneself. In face of these tensions, only contemplative waiting upon God makes it possible to preserve that inner vitality which comes from our love of the Church, the Body of Christ. In order not to become involved in useless discussions or in justifications which satisfy no one, and especially in order to keep alive that vision of the needs of the contemporary world, it is important that the will is steeped in the very sources of contemplation.

Whoever does not quench his thirst at these sources will find no serenity as he searches for the right attitude which will not definitely halt him on his way; so great is the danger that wrong attitudes may contaminate our life forces. There is the pressure of different kinds of conformity and the resistance to all change without which there can be no unity. There are some Churchmen who, while calling themselves good ecumenists, push the achievement of visible unity so far away that they exclude its possibility altogether. There are equally the narrow-minded men who, not from lack of culture, have an irresistible desire to put labels on their neighbour, to twist the meaning of his words, attempting by this means to break up the dialogue with other people. There are stupefyingly jealous people, who are a cancer in the Church of God. They search for compensation by neutralising the dynamism of new ventures. Did not Bernanos write that all spiritual adventures are a path to Calvary?

Each path of reconciliation demands that we constantly go yet further. Those who are committed to this path cannot avoid trials, even if they are tempted sometimes to escape from them.

Some people, it is true, are disturbed and deeply wounded by all that is implied by the ecumenical commitment. If the witnesses of unity disturb a Christian of their own confessional family, all will be well in spite of them; their vocation is to unite and pacify.

God gives a place of peace and joy to every Christian community in order that they should rest on Him alone, and go through the days of trials as well as the days of joy. Conversation with God inflames our zeal. It takes place in the Communion of all the Saints, witnesses of Christ, living or departed. It is preparation and nourishment for communication with all men by enabling us to radiate God and to be bearers of peace.

When I, with two of my brothers, met Pope John XXIII for the last time, he explained to us his way of making decisions, in a very simple prayer, in tranquillity, in speaking with God: "I speak with God," he said, and then added at once: "Oh! but quite humbly, quite simply."

When a man speaks with God, he is not looking for extraordinary revelations. He knows that for himself as for others, the most important thing is peace. Not a peace acquired once and for all, since the weight of our own character remains, the badly healed wounds where all sorts of contradictory feelings are in turmoil: bitterness, the passions which well up in our flesh, the illusions of an impossible love, or the unsatisfied longing of a disappointed love. All these things weigh us down and pull us to pieces, but the peace of Christ can reach to the depths, even to the wounded depths of our being.

Peace is not an inner passivity, nor a flight from our neighbour. The peace of Christ, and the insipid tranquillity in which horizons are narrowed down and gradually hem in the one who is enclosed within it, have nothing in common.

There is no peace where our neighbour is forgotten. Every day the same question is repeated: What have you done with your brother? The peace which does not foster communication and unity between brethren is nothing but an illusion. The man who has found peace is drawn to his neighbour; he encourages reconciliation and peace between those who are separated.

The peace of Christ needs time to grow to maturity, for it heals trials and suffering. But these things no longer overflow; they are kept and contained within us, and their hidden presence is a stimulation to our life forces.

A man of peace is himself a prefiguration of unanimity. He draws others along with him.

Bearers of ecumenicity

At Taizé, we have found that commitment to the chastity of celibacy is intimately bound up with our contemplative waiting upon God. How else can we make genuine the sign of a love for God which wants to be undivided?

When I master my body and keep it in obedience,[11] subjecting it to myself by vigils, by prayer, and by work, I do this solely out of love of Christ Jesus. He alone can sustain such a venture.

In its rejection of monasticism, the Reformation struck a blow against celibacy. It is surprising to discover that for centuries the Churches of the Reformation conspired to silence on the biblical texts dealing with celibacy. They acknowledge it in exceptional cases for greater availability. But the expectation of the coming of Christ as the principal motive of chastity, and celibacy as a sign of the Kingdom at hand, no longer appear in the thought of the Churches of the Reformation.

Luther's break with the monastic vows resulted not

only in the abolition of community life in Protestantism, but also in the almost complete disappearance of the vocation and the commitment to chastity. When criticising a position, men tend to caricature it. Particular cases of immorality were generalised, and because of this the call of the Gospel was for centuries discredited.

Today men who are committed to life in community, or to the priesthood, seek to find a confirmation of the call to chastity in our existence at Taizé, since there was no obligation which turned us in this direction. If there is a solidarity between us, it is precisely in this common venture to convey authentically the mysterious call of Christ. God designates those men as ambassadors of Christ who, despite all the limitations inseparable from our human existence, answer Him with the Yes and Amen of a faithful heart.

Chastity opens up an unsuspected ecumenical dimension: in this way of life, we mean to be men with hands so wholly outstretched towards hope in God, that we no longer want to keep anything for ourselves. This involves an exercise of openness to the universal, which allows us with a free heart to take up all the cares, everything which comes to us.

God gives the man who does not found a family according to the flesh an openness of heart and mind towards every family, human and spiritual. The man who for Christ's sake and that of the Gospel holds his arms open to all is able to live universal demands, and so to enter into every human situation. It becomes possible for the man who, in seeking God, wishes to be a man of a single love, to make the hidden presence of Christ felt even for men who cannot believe.

What has been said here represents a discovery which we have made at Taizé, and would seem to be exclusive in relation to marriage. But one can never say too often that celibacy inevitably helps to put the vocation to marriage in its true light. Fidelity in the bonds of marriage also means living in expectation of God. The conjugal community contains in miniature so many of the qualities of the Church. Some of the Church Fathers spoke of the family as a "little Church". Those who every day struggle to remain faithful in the indissoluble unity of marriage are also bearers of ecumenicity.

Intimacy and solitude

A large part of man's energy is spent in attempting to live emotional life to the full. Man is eagerly searching for intimacy with other human beings. And his search impels him to seek human relations without barriers and a communication without reserves. Intimacy appears as a goal without which there will be no happiness on earth, and its image is glorified as no other.

Every descent into one's self leads to the conclusion that each intimate relationship, even for the couple most at one, presupposes limitations. Beyond it, there is human solitude. He who rejects the natural order at this point will know the revolt which follows this rejection.

Acceptance of this fundamental solitude opens a way of peace, and makes possible for the Christian the discovery of an unknown dimension in his relationship with God. To accept this measure of solitude, this condition of all human life, stimulates intimacy with Him who rescues us from the overwhelming solitude of man faced with himself.

Saying to Christ "I love you", prompts us to manifest our intention to Him by a gesture, an action without which the word would remain a dead letter. It is for Him, in every struggle, to break in us that which must be broken, even if we are momentarily stricken in all our life forces. Intimacy with Him will fill up our solitude henceforth to be inhabited. Intimacy with Him will be communion, and will support a faith capable of moving mountains.

Contemplative expectation

The contemplative life is not an existence hovering

between heaven and earth, in ecstasy or revelations. It begins with a humble drawing near to God and to our neighbour. It always bears the seal of one who gets things done.

It makes a demand: to maintain the inner silence in all things. In order to do this, whether at work or alone, we must come back constantly to the short and frequent invocation of the name of Jesus, to psalms learnt by heart or sung, and to the simple gesture of the sign of the cross.

A contemplative life also means a way of looking at our neighbour; a way of looking which is transfigured by reconciliation. Those who continually see different faces pass before their eyes, are re-created by these, the creatures of God. Weariness itself is taken away, in the measure that they are welcomed with an attention constantly renewed at the sources of contemplation.

Through our contemplative expectation of God, we enter into those acts of acceptance which are necessary every day; acceptance of our situation in life, of our growing old, of lost opportunities, and of failures. Regret itself is transformed into a positive act, repentance, which gives new power to our movement forward.

In *Thomas Gordeieff*, Gorki tells of how Ignatius' boat is destroyed by ice on the Volga. Although a miser and watching every rouble, he at once accepts this loss. He realises that regrets would be in vain, and already begins to reassure himself with the thought of building a new boat.

In regret, the inner man disintegrates. The human spirit, far from being invigorated, becomes sterile when it drags itself through thoughts which uselessly reconstruct a bygone situation.

There are some childhoods which are invitations to an unconscious remorse. One always wants to start all over again in order to do better. But what work is there that we do really well? We always move in the realm of the pretty near. Regrets kill the creative impulse. Regrets are debilitating. If we are given a moment of certainty, of security, a sure standing ground, it is when we come together to wait upon God. Then everything becomes possible again, the salt regains its savour, that which had grown insipid acquires a wholly new meaning.

In contemplative expectation of God, all the pessimism which clings to us is dissolved, even if this pessimism has valid reasons for being there in what we see of the contemporary world and of ourselves.

There are so many reasons for pessimism in the world. There are those ever-growing masses of people, deprived of the sense of God, and those Christian societies turned in on themselves, which in Europe have known centuries of fratricidal strife. There is the prospect in twenty years' time of seeing four thousand million underdeveloped people, as against one thousand million well-fed. There is that immense wave which is slowly breaking over us: a technological civilisation which encompasses man and totally submerges him.

There are also many inner motives for discouragement: the struggle which we carry on day by day, the old self who will not submit, that pride of life, that hardness of will which refuses to take account of our neighbour, that despondency of fatigue. So many reasons for pessimism in our lives!

In contemplative expectation of God, all things become desirable again. Pessimism is dissolved and gives way to the optimism of faith. Then alone is it possible to appreciate what is coming to us, to welcome the events which today brings us, to hasten towards our neighbour, to set out afresh, to press forward. Only in contemplative expectation of God can we recover our lost impetus.

Wait—in expectancy!

Await the dawn of the life where God will gather us forever into himself.

Await within yourself and in others the event of God.

Await the unity of the Church, and through it the unity of all men.

Await the springtime of the Church.

Await above all and despite all the spirit of mercy, for a love which is not consuming is not charity, and without it we would profess an ecumenism without hope.

God is preparing a new Pentecost for us which will kindle all men with the fire of his love. It is for us to hasten towards the Event which will upset all our human prophecies, and restore life to our dry bones.

Let us hasten forwards, and not run away!

Let us hasten forwards to meet mankind's tomorrow, a technical civilisation charged with potential for human progress.

Let us hasten towards those who cannot believe and towards the world of the poor, a treasure which is waiting for us.

Let us hasten constantly and every moment to ask, to beg, to exhort to unity, and to raise up the sure sign of our brotherly love in the world of men and to reanimate unity from within.

Let us hasten towards institutions grown weary through time, to support their reforms, and to put everything in motion so that the tide of ecumenism may not ebb away.

NOTES

1. Psalm 22.7.
2. Colossians 3.12
3. Matthew 21.31
4. Acts 3.6.
5. Philippians 3.12.
6. Galatians 6.2.
7. *Weimar Ausgabe*, vol. II, p. 605.
8. Instruction of Pope Adrian VI to the Nuncio F. Chieregati in *Quellen zur Geschichte des Papsttums und des römischen Katholizismus*, 5th edn. Tübingen 1934, p. 261
9. Peter the Venerable, *Sermon sur la louange du Sépulcre du Seigneur Revue Benedictine*, 1954, p. 242.
10. Saint Bernard, letter 254, *Patrologie latine*, vol. 182, p. 461.
11. I Corinthians 9.27.